# The Seven Fairy Mountains of Cappadocia

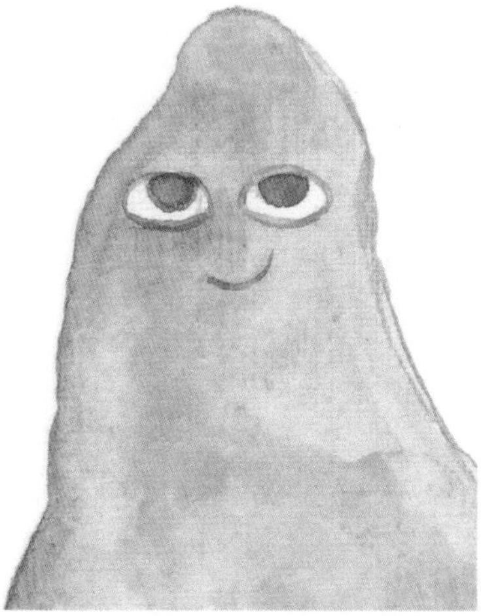

*Dedicated to my brother*

*Frank,*

*with love.*

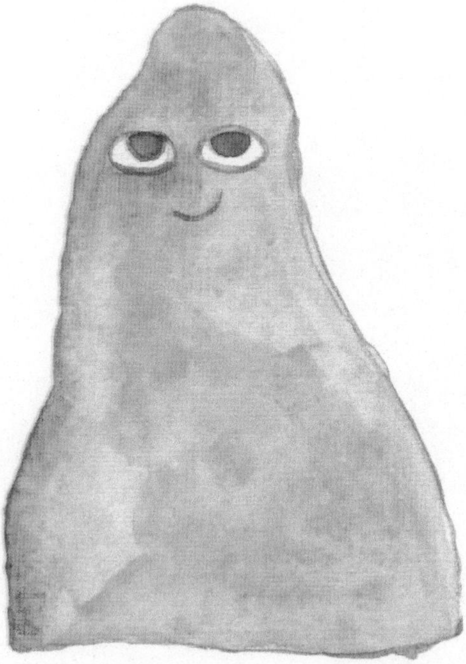

The Seven Fairy Mountains of Cappadocia
A Twinkle Truth Picture Book

Author Linda Socha Jaworski
Illustrator Serpil Ural
Turkish Lanugage Consultant Serpil Ural
Technical Director Michael Jaworski
Editor Laura Jaworski
Photographer Linda Jaworski


Twinkle Truth Publications



'Laugh and trust,' He said. - A.J.Russell

Once upon a time, long, long ago, there dwelt a cozy group of seven fairy mountains. They lived in the land of Cappadocia in the town of Göreme; the ancient region of Asia Minor and present day East Central Turkey. Of those seven cozy fairy mountains of Göreme, six eventually became homes to artistic families! The families named their town 'Seven Fairy Mountain Village.'

Küçük, the smallest and youngest fairy mountain, watched with delight as smoke puffed from her six sisters' hewn chimneys. She could smell savory lentil soup, pita baking and lamb grilling. The inhabitants of this comfy village were snug in their fairy mountain homes and busy with budding businesses. Even though Küçük longed to have a family of her own, she felt warm and cozy too.

Throughout the nighttimes when all was quiet in the fairy mountains of Göreme, the sisters would share stories of what had happened during their busy days.

Sister Parlak laughed merrily as the children climbed throughout her mountain rooms. She loved her human family and found that her life as a home was indeed fulfilling.

Sister Pürüzsüz giggled heartily as her family painted enriching Turkish frescoes here, there and everywhere. She loved her human family and found that her life as a home was indeed fulfilling.

Sister Uzun Boylu glimmered gently as stairs hewn throughout her rooms drummed with little feet that ran from top to bottom all day long. She loved her human family and found that her life as a home was indeed fulfilling.

Sister Hoşgeldiniz grinned festively as her oddly shaped rooms were fancily decorated in beautiful shades of blue. She loved her human family and found that her life as a home was indeed fulfilling.

Sister Kubbe shimmered jollily as her family filled her rooms with musical notes of enchanting melodies. She loved her human family and found that her life as a home was indeed fulfilling.

Sister Üstü Düz beamed pleasantly as delectable smells of Turkish cooking filled the air throughout her rooms. She loved her human family and found that her life as a home was indeed fulfilling.

Little Küçük beamed with admiration and pride to see busy families thriving in her sister fairy mountain homes. Küçük loved her happy little town, but wondered why she had no human family of her own. It might be because of the large grubby sphere held fast in the middle of Küçük's floor! Perhaps there was not enough space left around the object to make a home. And there were cracks! Because of her size, rains and erosion had been harder on little Küçük than they had been on her sisters. Dear little Küçük had so many troubles!

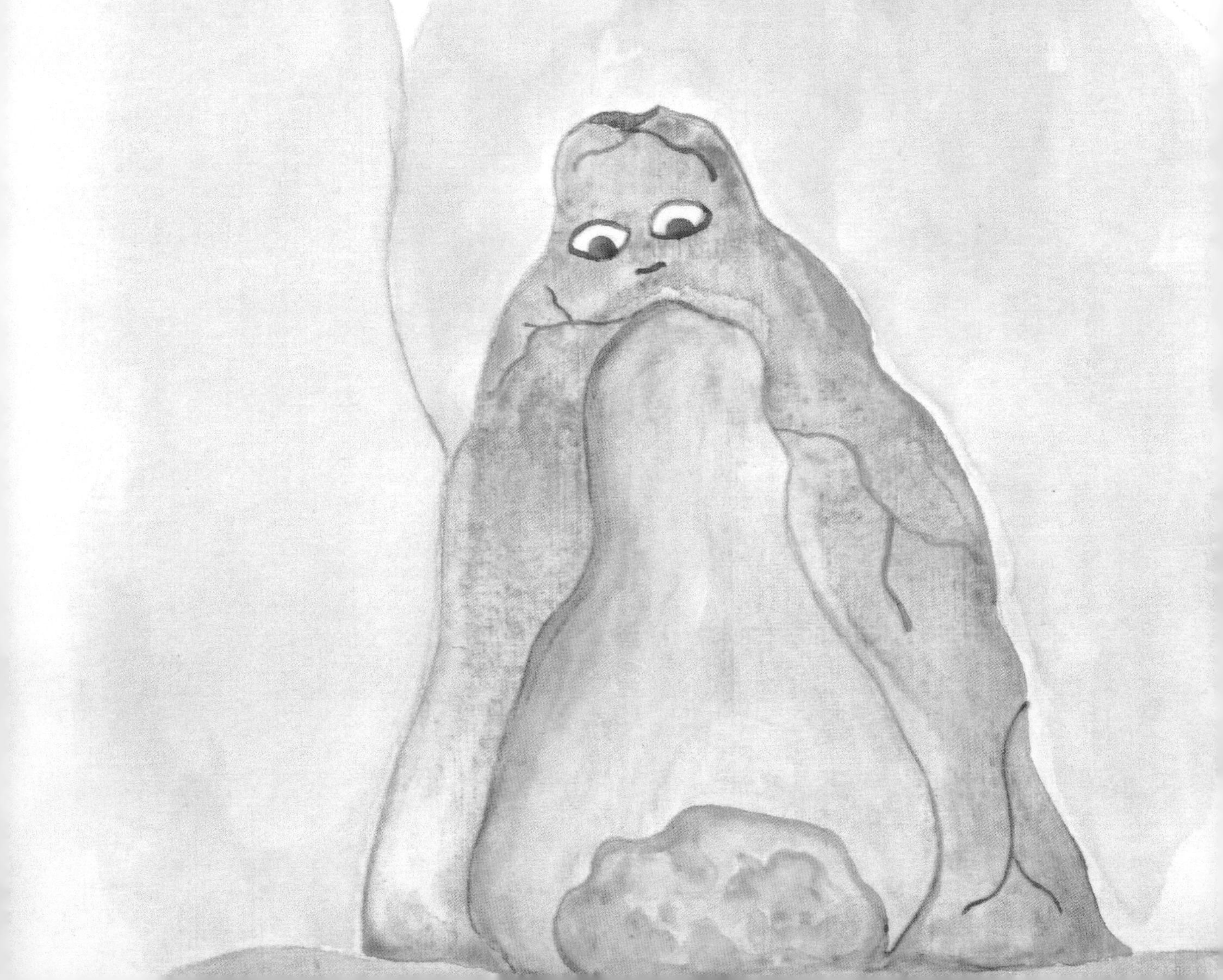

Though each family had a business, travelers and customers were rare. Küçük privately worried that her poor condition was the cause, and wished that somehow she could become a welcoming mountain like her sisters.

Parlak's first floor was a clothing shop. The clothing was exceptionally boutique! Nevertheless, customers were scarce and the family just barely eked out a living.

Pürüzsüz's first floor was an art gallery. The whole family created the most exquisite, bright and cheerful paintings. Nevertheless, customers were scarce and the family just barely eked out a living.

Uzun Boylu's first floor was a nursery. The family provided a nurturing environment for children! Nevertheless, customers were scarce and the family just barely eked out a living.

Hoşgeldiniz's first floor was for visitors to book accommodations to stay in her home-hotel. The rooms available on her second and third levels were lovely, cozy and warm! Nevertheless, customers were scarce and the family just barely eked out a living.

Kubbe's first floor was a music shop. Wonderful music teachers gave lessons, handcrafted musical instruments were for sale, and the concerts in the dome were melodiously inspiring. Nevertheless, customers were scarce and the family just barely eked out a living.

Üstü Düz's first floor and rooftop terrace were a marvelous Turkish restaurant. Travelers could feast on delicious food while enjoying the glorious view. Nevertheless, customers were scarce and the family just barely eked out a living.

No one could quite figure out why, but the lovely little village could not attract enough customers.

Küçük often thought about how much she wanted to be a home for a family. She felt worried about the wind and rain that continued to erode her tiptop and wished she could find a way to repair the damage. Rain found its pathways through Küçük's cracks all too often.

Little Küçük watched the trickle of visitors diminish and felt very sad. She had an awful lot of worries.

Each night, Küçük would fix her gaze upon the shiniest star and wish,

"Five points, yonder far,
I make my wish upon that star,
I wish for a family, just for me,
To become the home, I know I can be."

One cool summer night, the townsfolk sat outside looking up at the stars. Oil for their lamps was expensive, so they chose starlight as their guide. Wishing on stars was a custom in Seven Fairy Mountain Village. That evening, there was one star in particular that was so bright that everyone admired it; one might wonder if they all wished on the very same twinkling star! It became late so everyone went home and retired for the night.

Several hours later, a weary traveler on his way to Kavak happened by Seven Fairy Mountain Village. Mehmet the potter was traveling through Pigeon Valley to collect special clay for his pottery. Chilled and tired, Mehmet stopped in front of the Hoşgeldiniz Hotel. It was terribly dark and quiet; Mehmet felt obliged not to bother the hotel proprietor and guests. He was so tired that he thought he would just lie on the ground to sleep, when a waft of warm air touched his face as it floated upon the night's breeze. Surprised and excited, Mehmet searched for the source. He followed the warm air to Küçük's mountain entrance.

Moonlight flowed into Küçük through her tiptop. The light allowed Mehmet to see the the strange, uncommon object in the middle of her floor. It was radiating such warmth that he was drawn to it. Mehmet pulled a blanket from his satchel and snuggled himself near the warmth, and before long he fell into an enchanted and welcomed sleep.

Küçük was feeling oh so glorious; she had a visitor and it was delightful!

Mehmet awakened feeling rested and refreshed. He sat there marveling at this little mountain's rarity and realized that Küçük's curious object held the sun's warmth! Mesmerized and excited about his discovery, a grand idea burst into Mehmet's mind!

Mehmet the potter decided Küçük would make a perfect home for him and his family! He scrubbed the sun catcher in the middle of Küçük's floor until a beautiful ball of iron was revealed! He repaired Küçük's cracks using his clay pottery. Mehmet crafted clay drains so the rainwater would flow into vessels fitted around the sun catcher. The heat of the metal warmed the collected rainwater and created a lovely steam bath; the first hamam was born in Seven Fairy Mountain Village!

Küçük's location was perfect for Mehmet: he was close to the clay basins of Kavak and the backyard was ideal for a potter's wheel and tubs of clay! As a result of Mehmet's self-heating hamam, visitors began to come! Little Küçük became a thriving business-home for Mehmet.

Mehmet's family was so happy about moving into their very own fairy mountain! Küçük loved her human family and found that her life as a home was indeed fulfilling.

Everyone had always loved Küçük just they way she was, but Küçük had longed for her own human family. Her sisters felt such gladness that not only had she gotten her wish, but had brought a new specialty to their village as well!

Good news travels! Summertime at the Seven Fairy Mountain Village became filled with the hustle and bustle of a busy, thriving town. It seemed that a pottery shop and hamam were exactly what were needed to make the village just right. Tales of Küçük's sun catcher were told far and wide! One traveler decided that the iron sphere arrived from a celestial place, another reported that it was a broken piece of the earth's core, and yet another said it was a rare metal flower! Everyone wanted to see it!

Uzun Boylu’s family was busy singing and dancing with all the playful little children!

Pürüzsüz’s family was busy brushing marvelous paintings for all the art collectors!

Parlak's family was busy designing unique clothing for all the fashion seekers!

Kubbe's family was busy composing joyful melodies for music lovers!

Hoşgeldiniz's family was busy decorating charming accommodations for all the weary travelers!

Üstü Düz's family was busy cooking scrumptious Turkish foods for all the hungry customers!

And, little Küçük was busy loving the warmth of the sunlight, the calm of the steam and the sounds of a potter's wheel with heartfelt pride in her village!

All the families from the Seven Fairy Mountain Village of Cappadocia lived happily ever after.

And so has the sun, as she still shines her warmth upon the Fairy Mountain homes of Cappadocia to this very day!

# Turkish Language Translation

| Sister's Name | Meaning | Pronunciation |
|---|---|---|
| Parlak | Bright | parr-lock |
| Pürüzsüz | Smooth | poo-rooz-sooz |
| Uzun Boylu | Tall | uhz-un-boyloo |
| Hoşgeldiniz | Welcome | hoe-sh-gell-deen-eez |
| Kubbe | Dome, cupola | kuh-bb-eh |
| Üstü Düz | Flat Top | oost-oo-dooz |
| Küçük | Small | kooch-ook |
| Hamam | Turkish Steam Bath | ha-mahm |

# Cappadocia

Cappadocia is located in the Central Anatolian region of Turkey. As a result of volcanic eruptions and river erosion, 'chimney rocks' were formed in the region. These rock formations are considered a wonder of nature, and are unique the world over! Dating back to the Bronze Age, Cappadocia was inhabited by Assyrian civilizations, as well as Hittite, Frig, Pers, Byzantine, Seljuk, and Ottoman civilizations. Underground cities were constructed from the volcanic rock as a means of protection from wildlife and the elements. Some of the tunnels connecting the underground rooms in these cities are so small that only one person can travel through at a time! Cappadocia is now a major tourism center in Turkey, and is visited by hundreds of thousands of tourists every year. If you would like to learn more about Cappadocia, check out this website to continue your investigation!

Information: Fodor's Turkey, 2007 by Fodor's Travel, Random House
http://www.cappadociaturkey.net/

# Cappadocia, Turkey
# December 2010

Printed in Great Britain
by Amazon

25587461R00023